Who Was
Marie Curie?

Who Was Marie Curie?

by Megan Stine

illustrated by Ted Hammond

Penguin Workshop

For my mother—MS

PENGUIN WORKSHOP
An Imprint of Penguin Random House LLC, New York

The publisher does not have any control over and does not assume any responsibility for author or third-party websites or their content.

Visit us online at www.penguinrandomhouse.com.

Library of Congress Control Number: 2014017364

ISBN 9780448478968   10 9 8 7 6 5 4 3 2

Part of the *What Is Science & Technology?* Boxed Set, ISBN 9780593090138

Contents

Who Was
Marie Curie?

One day in November 1903, Marie Curie and her husband got a letter in the mail. The letter invited them to travel from Paris to Sweden to meet the king and queen! Marie was about to be given a gold medal, a fancy dinner, and a huge amount of money. She was about to become famous all over the world. She was about to win the Nobel Prize!

What had she done to deserve all this?

Marie Curie was a scientist at a time when there were almost no female scientists. In fact, most women didn't even go to college then! Marie wasn't like most women. She spoke five languages. She loved math problems so much that her father sent them to her in his letters. She met Albert Einstein—the most famous scientist in the world! She was brilliant and determined to succeed.

Marie was being given the Nobel Prize for her work in science. She had discovered a new metal! She called it radium.

At first, Marie didn't even know what this new metal was. All she knew was that it was amazingly powerful. It gave off energy! It glowed in the dark, giving off a faint green light. Marie thought it looked like fairy light.

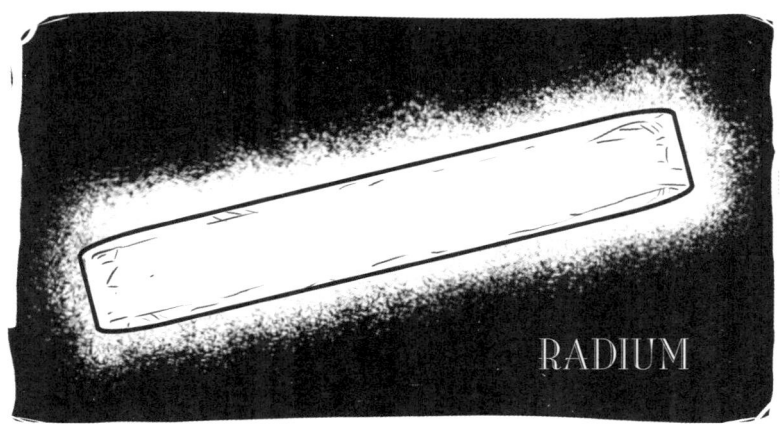

RADIUM

By the time her work was done, Marie's discovery would change the world in good ways and bad. Marie Curie would be the most famous woman scientist in history.

THE NOBEL PRIZE

THE NOBEL PRIZE IS ONE OF THE MOST FAMOUS AND IMPORTANT AWARDS GIVEN. IT WAS CREATED BY THE SWEDISH SCIENTIST WHO INVENTED DYNAMITE. ALFRED NOBEL WAS VERY RICH. HE WANTED TO REWARD PEOPLE WHO HELPED MAKE THE WORLD A BETTER PLACE. HE CREATED THE NOBEL PRIZE IN HIS WILL. THE PRIZES ARE GIVEN FOR SCIENCES, MEDICINE, LITERATURE, AND PEACE. IN 2013, EACH NOBEL PRIZE CAME WITH A CASH AWARD OF MORE THAN $1 MILLION!

THE WINNERS OF THE NOBEL PRIZE ARE INVITED TO COME TO STOCKHOLM, SWEDEN, FOR A FANCY CEREMONY. THERE, THEY ARE GIVEN A GOLD MEDAL BY THE KING OF SWEDEN! THEN A HUGE BANQUET IS HELD WITH THE KING AND QUEEN.

THE VERY FIRST NOBEL PRIZES WERE GIVEN IN 1901. ONE OF THE SCIENCE PRIZES WAS GIVEN TO WILHELM RÖNTGEN, THE MAN WHO DISCOVERED X-RAYS. MARIE AND PIERRE CURIE WON IN 1903. OTHER FAMOUS WINNERS INCLUDE ALBERT EINSTEIN, MARTIN LUTHER KING JR., BARACK OBAMA, JIMMY CARTER, AND AL GORE.

ALFR. NOBEL

NAT. MDCCC XXXIII OB. MDCCC XCVI

Chapter 1
Eager to Learn

Maria Sklodowska was born on November 7, 1867. She was the youngest of five children, with three older sisters and one brother. Her parents were both teachers. Her mother was the principal of a school. Her father taught science. Later, he ran his own schools.

Maria was born in Warsaw, the capital city of Poland. Poland didn't really exist as a country at that time. The neighboring countries had taken over Poland and divided it up into three parts. Maria lived in the part that was ruled by Russia.

Russian guards walked the streets where Maria

lived, and patrolled the schools where her parents taught. The Russians had strict rules. No one could sing Polish songs. Schools weren't allowed to teach Polish history. Students and teachers couldn't even speak Polish! All the classes had to be taught in Russian.

Maria's family hated the Russians and hated the rules. Her father was very proud to be Polish. He taught his children to love their country and hate the Russians. When Maria and her friend walked past a Russian statue, they spat on it!

Maria was a wonderful, bright, and curious child. At age four, she loved to stare into a glass case that held her father's science equipment. She adored her father and listened intently to everything he said. Her father turned every conversation into a lesson. He created games to teach his children geography. He gave them math problems. He read poems aloud. He spoke five languages, and Maria learned to speak them, too.

At school, Maria was the smartest girl in her class. She could recite all the right answers in either Polish or Russian. When the Russian guards weren't around, the teachers were sneaky. They taught classes in Polish.

One day a Russian guard came to visit.
Quickly, the whole class switched back to
speaking Russian. Everyone felt nervous. If the
guards found out the truth, they might punish
people. They might send them away to a cold,
distant place in Russia called Siberia.

The teacher called on Maria to answer
questions in Russian for the guard. Maria passed
the test brilliantly, but she felt bad for doing it!

She felt like a traitor to her country for obeying
the Russians.

Life was hard for Maria's family. Her mother was very sick with a disease called tuberculosis. She had to go away for more than a year to try to get well.

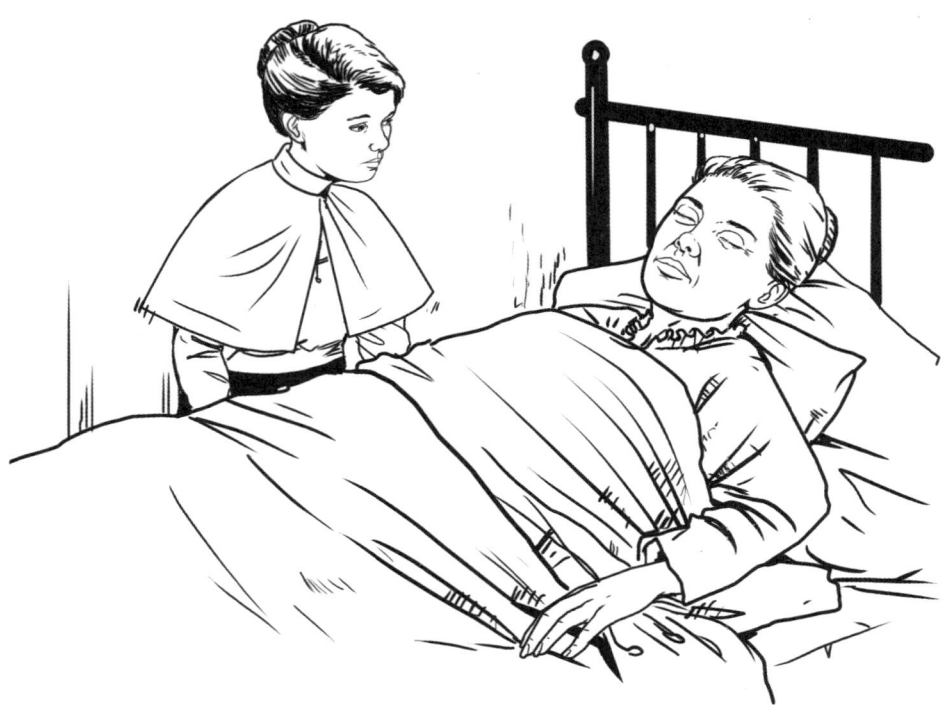

Soon after, her father was fired from his job at a Russian school. To make money, he started a boarding school at home. More than twenty

boys came each day. Some of them lived with the
family. Others just came to study. The house was
crowded, noisy, and not very clean.

The crowding made it more likely that people would get sick. Maria's sister Zofia got a disease called typhus and died. Four years later, Maria's mother died. Maria became deeply sad.

At the end of the school year, Maria's teacher told her father that Maria was stressed out. The teacher thought Maria should take a year off from school. Instead, her father sent her to a tough Russian school. In Maria's family, no one ever took a break from learning.

In 1883, Maria graduated first in her class at the age of fifteen. She even got the school's gold medal for being the best student!

After high school, Maria's father agreed to let his daughter have a break. Maria was too young to get married, and her father could not afford to send her to college. Instead, he sent her to live with relatives in the countryside.

For the next year, Maria lived a wonderful, carefree life. Her uncles played music, took her to

dances, and invited all kinds of interesting guests to the house. Many days, Maria slept late and then played outside like a child. She loved swinging, collecting wild berries, fishing, reading, and playing games. At night she went to parties and learned a Polish dance called the mazurka.

She felt so free! In the countryside, she later wrote, she could even "sing patriotic songs without going to prison."

It was the happiest time she had ever had in her young life.

Chapter 2
The Secret School

Rested and older now, Maria was eager to start college, but there was only enough money in the family for one student at a time. Her brother Jozef was already in medical school. Maria and her sisters would have to wait their turns. Besides, Warsaw University didn't let girls in!

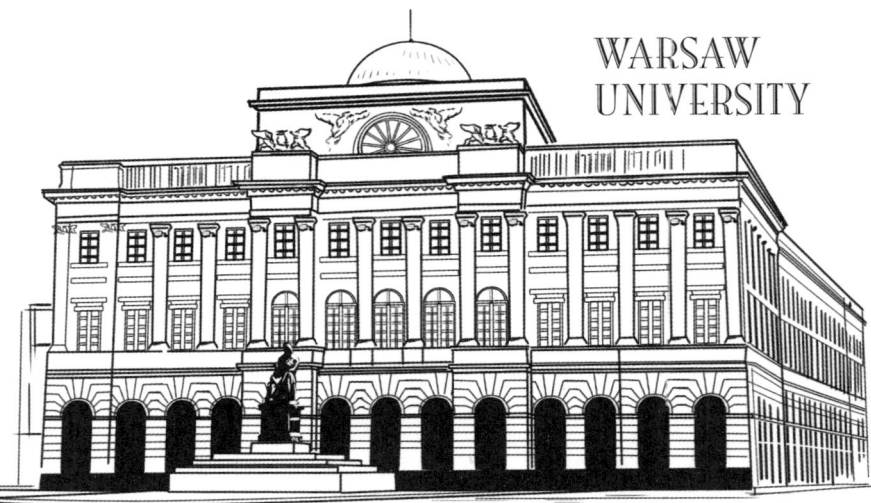

WARSAW
UNIVERSITY

For the next year, Maria decided to study on her own. She longed to be a scientist like her father. How would she ever learn science without teachers and laboratories and classrooms?

Luckily, there was a very clever woman who could help. The woman's name was Jadwiga Dawidowa. Jadwiga knew that many young Polish women wanted to study, even if it meant risking punishment and breaking the Russian rules. Jadwiga started a secret university!

JADWIGA DAWIDOWA

At first, the classes were taught in private homes. The smartest scientists and writers in Warsaw volunteered to teach. Later, Jadwiga secretly moved the classes to bigger buildings. The classes had to keep moving—

flying from place to place—so the Russian police wouldn't find out. Soon it became known as the Flying University!

Maria and her sister Bronia took classes at the Flying University.

Still, they both dreamed of attending a real university someday, but where? The best choice was the Sorbonne, a famous university in Paris, France. It was probably the best school in Europe, and it accepted women.

THE SORBONNE

Maria and Bronia came up with a plan. They would take turns! Bronia would go to Paris first to study. Maria would stay in Poland to earn money for them both. After Bronia graduated from the Sorbonne, it would be Maria's turn.

Maria took a job as a governess. At the age of eighteen, she left her beloved father and home behind to live with a rich family in the countryside. Her job as governess was to teach the

children in that family. One of her students was a girl a year older than Maria!

At first, Maria liked the job. She had her own big room. There was plenty of food and the parents were kind to her. They invited her to parties and treated her almost like a member of the family. In her free time, she read math and science books.

One day, something happened that changed
everything. Maria met the oldest son in the family.
His name was Kazimierz, or Kaz for short. Maria

and Kaz fell in love, but when his family found out, they forbade him to marry her. Why? Because she was only a governess! Even though she was smart, educated, and had good manners, they thought she was more like a servant. She wasn't good enough to marry their son.

From that moment on, Maria was miserable. She hated living and working for people who looked down on her, but she had to keep her pledge to Bronia. For another year or more, she kept the job, hating it all the time.

After that, Maria worked as a governess for another family, then she returned home to study at the Flying University again.

Finally her sister Bronia wrote to her from Paris. Bronia had finished her schooling and had married a man who happened to have the same name as Maria's old boyfriend—Kazimierz! Bronia and her Kaz invited Maria to come live with them so she could attend the Sorbonne.

In 1891, Maria boarded a train for Paris. When she arrived, she would begin to use a new name—Marie. It was the French version of Maria.

A whole new life was about to begin.

Chapter 3
Hungry But Happy

The train trip to Paris took three days. Marie couldn't pay for a seat. She rode the whole way on a stool that she brought with her! The train car was so cold, she kept herself wrapped in blankets.

She barely had enough food to eat during the trip.
It was just the first of many hardships that would
soon be part of her everyday life.

Marie didn't care, though. She was happy to
be finally fulfilling her dream. The Sorbonne was
such a different kind of place. There were
almost no rules. She could take
whatever classes she wanted.
She didn't have to attend class
if she didn't feel like it. She
could even choose whether
or not to take tests!
Best of all, the
tuition was free.

Living with
Bronia was not so
much fun, though.
Bronia and Kaz
were both doctors.
Their patients came

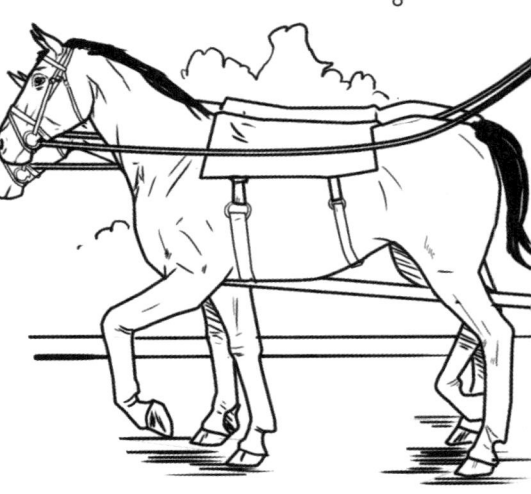

to the apartment for treatment. The house was always crowded and noisy. Marie's trip to the Sorbonne every day was a long one. She had to ride in the cold, on the top deck of an open bus, an hour each way.

After six months, Marie moved out and rented her own place closer to the Sorbonne. Her apartment was a tiny single room on the top floor of an apartment building. She had no kitchen, so she did all her cooking over an alcohol lamp!

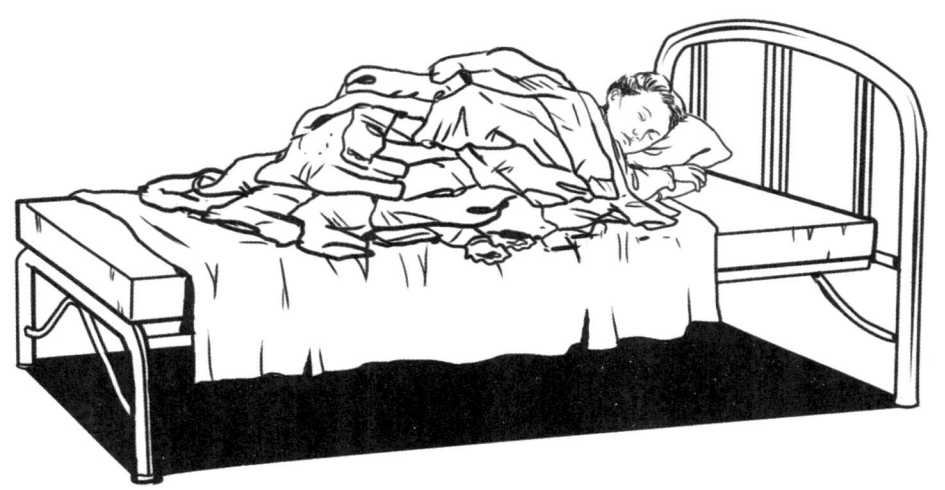

Her meals were skimpy—just bread with maybe a cup of hot chocolate, an egg, or fruit. One time, Marie was so hungry that she fainted while studying in the library.

In winter, her room was so cold that water would freeze in a bowl! If she wanted heat, she had to buy coal and carry it up six flights of stairs. She couldn't always afford coal. Most of the time she slept with all her clothes piled on top of her, to keep warm!

It was a hard time for a woman to live alone in Paris. Very few women went to college. When Marie entered the science department at the Sorbonne, there were 1,825 students—but only twenty-three of them were women! There were so few women studying in France that the French didn't even have a word for "female student." The only word they had meant "girlfriend of a student."

Marie spoke French but not very well at first. She had to work hard to understand French people and to make sure she pronounced words correctly.

Still, Marie was happy. Years later, she called it one of the

best memories of her life. She loved her classes, and spent every waking minute studying. She didn't care about anything except science, and she was being taught by some of the most famous scientists in all of Europe. One of her professors, Gabriel Lippmann, would later win a Nobel Prize for inventing a way to make color photographs.

After three years of hard work and constant study, Marie took her final exams in science.

GABRIEL LIPPMANN

Only two women graduated that year. Marie was first in her whole class—ahead of all the men!

Now that she was finished studying, Marie thought she would go home to Poland. She had promised her father to come back and take care of him.

Then something lucky happened. She got a scholarship to stay another year. This time she would study math! Marie couldn't resist. Learning was the most satisfying thing she had ever done in her life. Why would she want to stop now?

Chapter 4
Two Loves

For the next year, Marie studied math at the Sorbonne. When she took her exams, she came in second in the class!

Was it time now to go back to Poland as she had promised?

Not quite yet. Marie's professor, Gabriel Lippmann, found her a job in a lab at the Sorbonne. Her task was to study magnetism and steel.

Magnetism is the force that causes magnets and metal to stick together. It was perfect for Marie—she was always happiest doing experiments. There was only one problem—the lab didn't have the best equipment. Marie struggled with her experiments. She couldn't get good results.

To help her, some friends from Poland

PIERRE CURIE

introduced Marie to a Frenchman named Pierre Curie. Pierre was a scientist who had become famous at a very young age. When Pierre was twenty-one, he and his brother had discovered that quartz crystals could hold an electrical charge. After that, he invented a scientific tool called an electrometer. It was used to measure very small amounts of

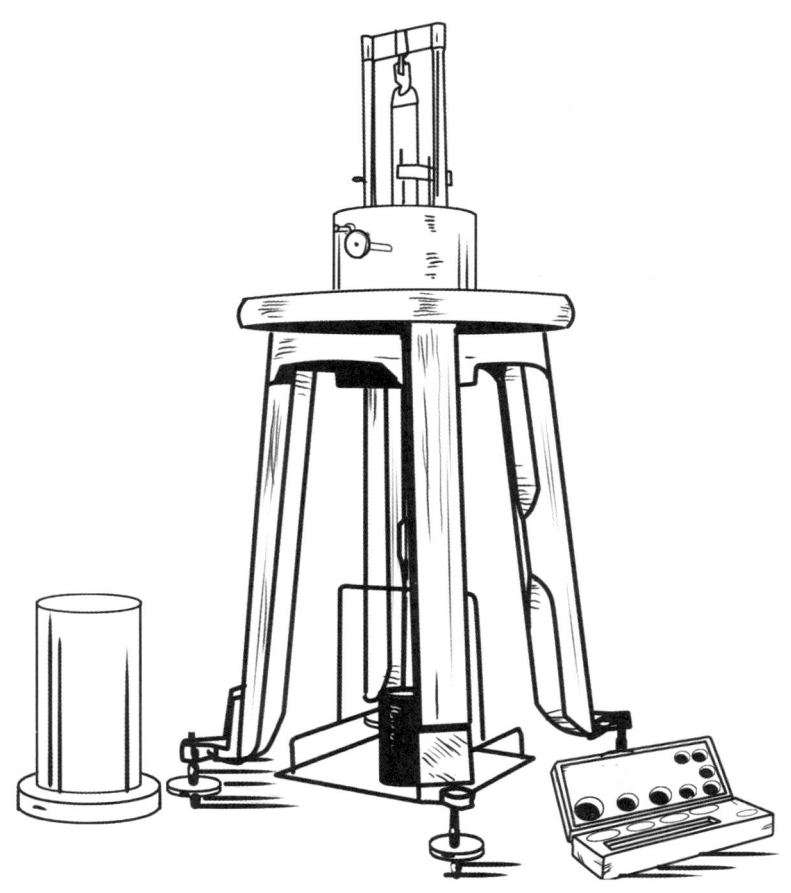

electricity. Marie needed his electrometer for her experiments.

The day Marie met Pierre, her whole life changed. Until then, she had thought she would never fall in love again. She thought it didn't matter. She was planning to devote her life solely to science. But Pierre was so special, so different from other men. He was smart, quiet, and he loved science as much as she did. In so many ways, he was just like Marie.

Pierre had been brought up in a family just like Marie's, too. His father was a doctor and scientist. His parents thought education was extremely important—just like Marie's. Unlike Marie, Pierre had had trouble learning in school, so his parents taught him at home. They let him find his own way. When he discovered how much he liked math and science, he went from being a slow learner to being super fast.

By the time Pierre was twenty-three years old he was teaching college!

The minute Marie and Pierre met, they each knew that the other was special. Pierre felt he had found a "woman of genius." Marie knew that

Pierre was the kind of man she could talk to and trust. She invited him to her tiny room to discuss science and sip tea.

Very soon, Pierre was in love with Marie.

He wanted to marry her, but Marie was not so sure. In the summer of 1894, she went home to Warsaw. Her heart had been broken once by Kaz. She wasn't ready to take another chance on love.

Pierre wouldn't give up, though. He wrote to her and begged her to come back to Paris to be with him. He even offered to leave France—a country he loved—and come live in Poland.

Finally Marie realized Pierre truly loved her and that they could have a life together as scientists. The two of them were married in France on July 26, 1895. On a perfect summer day, the wedding reception was held in his parents' garden. Wonderful food was served, including a huge turkey and giant peaches! After they ate, the guests played a French ball game on the lawn. It was a happy occasion in every way.

For their honeymoon, they bought two bicycles and rode off on a long adventure. Their honeymoon bike trip lasted all summer long!

When they came back to Paris in the fall,
they quickly got to work. Nothing made them
happier than spending all day—and even all
night—in a lab.

Chapter 5
Marie's Discovery

For the next few years, Marie kept studying. At the same time, she kept her job doing research in magnetism.

Meanwhile, she enjoyed her life with Pierre. She bought fresh flowers each week for their apartment. She learned to make jelly from gooseberries. She and Pierre rode their bicycles everywhere. They fell more and more in love.

On September 12, 1897, Marie and Pierre had a baby girl. They named her Irene.

When the baby was a few months old, Pierre's father moved in with them. His wife had just died, and he was alone. He was willing to help take care of his granddaughter. Marie was glad

because she was ready to get back to work.

In those days, women almost never worked outside of the home, but Marie was different. She wanted to do some important research so that she could get her PhD—the degree that would make her a professor.

The only question now was: What should she work on?

Marie and Pierre lived during an exciting time in Paris. The whole world was going crazy for a new scientific discovery—X-rays! The mysterious X-rays had just been discovered two years earlier. Scientists were trying to figure out how X-rays really worked. They soon noticed that X-rays could make some things glow in the dark.

But Marie wanted to study a topic of her own. She decided to study a different kind of rays, called Becquerel rays. These rays were named for Henri Becquerel, the man who discovered them. The rays came from a metal called uranium.

HENRI BECQUEREL

HENRI BECQUEREL CAME FROM A FAMILY OF SCIENTISTS. BOTH HIS FATHER AND HIS GRANDFATHER WERE SCIENTISTS. THEY HAD STUDIED THINGS THAT WERE PHOSPHORESCENT— THINGS THAT GLOWED IN THE DARK.

HENRI FOLLOWED IN THEIR FOOTSTEPS. WITHOUT DOING MUCH WORK, HE WAS QUICKLY ADMITTED TO THE FRENCH ACADEMY OF SCIENCES. BECAUSE HENRI'S FATHER WAS FAMOUS, HENRI HAD AN EASY PATH TO SUCCESS.

HENRI EXPERIMENTED WITH X-RAYS AND URANIUM. HE DISCOVERED RADIOACTIVITY BEFORE MARIE CURIE DID, BUT BECQUEREL DIDN'T USE THE WORD *RADIOACTIVITY*. HE DIDN'T REALIZE THAT LOTS OF CHEMICALS COULD GIVE OFF ENERGY, AND HE DIDN'T COMPLETELY UNDERSTAND WHERE THE ENERGY WAS COMING FROM. BECQUEREL HELD ON TO THE IDEA THAT THE ENERGY HAD SOMETHING TO DO WITH PHOSPHORESCENCE.

AFTER HIS FIRST SUCCESS, HENRI STOPPED EXPERIMENTING WITH URANIUM. THAT'S ONE REASON MARIE CURIE DECIDED TO PICK IT UP.

Today we know that uranium is one of several metals that give off powerful radioactive rays. But when Marie Curie started her research, the word *radioactive* didn't even exist! No one knew why uranium gave off energy or why it could make things glow in the dark. No one knew then that uranium could be used to make a bomb or a nuclear power plant. Marie's research was going to open the door for all that knowledge.

Marie set up a laboratory with Pierre's help. They shared the lab together. It was cold and grungy—just an old storage room in the school where Pierre taught. Marie didn't mind. Work was all she cared about.

In the lab, Marie used Pierre's electrometer to measure rays coming from different metals. The tests were very tricky. She had to have very steady hands. No one else could do the tests as well as Marie. Even Becquerel had tried and failed!

At first, Marie tested uranium. Then she tested

other metals, including gold and copper. Only the uranium gave off rays.

Then Marie did something brilliant—something that would change science forever. She decided to test a rock called pitchblende. Pitchblende is a rock that contains a lot of uranium. But it has other metals in it, too.

When Marie tested the pitchblende, she found it gave off even *more* rays than uranium alone! How could that be? Marie figured out the answer. There had to be something else—another metal—mixed into the pitchblende!

PITCHBLENDE

That other metal, whatever it was, had even more energy than uranium.

Soon Marie realized the truth. She had discovered a new element that the world didn't know about!

Marie named the new metal after her homeland of Poland. She called it polonium. Then she came up with a word for the rays that the metals gave off. She called it "radioactivity." It meant that metals like polonium and uranium were able to release energy into the air.

WHAT IS AN ELEMENT?

EVERY PURE CHEMICAL IN THE WORLD IS CALLED AN *ELEMENT*. METALS SUCH AS COPPER, GOLD, AND URANIUM ARE ALL ELEMENTS. SO ARE GASES SUCH AS HELIUM—THE GAS INSIDE HELIUM BALLOONS. THE AIR WE BREATHE IS NOT AN ELEMENT BECAUSE IT ISN'T A SINGLE, PURE

The Periodic Table of

1 H								
3 Li	4 Be							
11 Na	12 Mg							
19 K	20 Ca	21 Sc	22 Ti	23 V	24 Cr	25 Mn	26 Fe	27 Co
37 Rb	38 Sr	39 Y	40 Zr	41 Nb	42 Mo	43 Tc	44 Ru	45 Rh
55 Cs	56 Ba	57-71	72 Hf	73 Ta	74 W	75 Re	76 Os	77 Ir
87 Fr	88 Ra	89-103	104 Rf	105 Db	106 Sg	107 Bh	108 Hs	109 Mt

Lanthanide Series	57 La	58 Ce	59 Pr	60 Nd	61 Pm	62 Sm	63 Eu
Actinide Series	89 Ac	90 Th	91 Pa	92 U	93 Np	94 Pu	95 Am

CHEMICAL. AIR IS A MIXTURE OF OXYGEN AND
OTHER ELEMENTS.

SCIENTISTS HAVE A CHART THAT TELLS THEM
WHAT ALL THE ELEMENTS IN THE WORLD ARE. SO
FAR, WE KNOW OF 118 ELEMENTS, BUT SCIENTISTS
STILL COULD DISCOVER MORE.

								2 He
Elements			5 B	6 C	7 N	8 O	9 F	10 Ne
			13 Al	14 Si	15 P	16 S	17 Cl	18 Ar
28 Ni	29 Cu	30 Zn	31 Ga	32 Ge	33 As	34 Se	35 Br	36 Kr
46 Pd	47 Ag	48 Cd	49 In	50 Sn	51 Sb	52 Te	53 I	54 Xe
78 Pt	79 Au	80 Hg	81 Tl	82 Pb	83 Bi	84 Po	85 At	86 Rn
110 Ds	111 Rg	112 Cn	113 Uut	114 Fl	115 Uup	116 Lv	117 Uus	118 Uuo
64 Gd	65 Tb	66 Dy	67 Ho	68 Er	69 Tm	70 Yb	71 Lu	
96 Cm	97 Bk	98 Cf	99 Es	100 Fm	101 Md	102 No	103 Lr	

To let the world know about her new discoveries, Marie did what scientists always do: She wrote a report. She wanted to read it to a group of other scientists in the Academy of Sciences in Paris.

The Academy was like a fancy science club for the most important scientists in France. It was hard to join and members had to be voted in.

Marie and Pierre were not members of the Academy. At that time, Pierre couldn't even get a job teaching at the Sorbonne! Other scientists thought Marie and Pierre weren't good enough because they didn't have PhDs from the best colleges. Besides, Marie was a woman. The Academy never let women in. Women weren't even allowed inside the Academy's rooms!

Luckily, though, Marie and Pierre had important friends. All the famous scientists in Europe and America knew one another. In April 1898, Marie's report about her discoveries was

read to the Academy by her teacher and friend Gabriel Lippmann.

The scientists were interested in Marie's report, but no one was amazed—not yet. They weren't sure she was right. Marie still had to prove that polonium existed. How? By separating it out of the pitchblende.

WHAT IS RADIOACTIVITY?

RADIOACTIVITY IS A SPECIAL KIND OF ENERGY THAT COMES FROM INSIDE THE ATOMS IN CERTAIN METALS OR CHEMICALS. WHEN SOMETHING IS RADIOACTIVE, IT GIVES OFF ENERGY RAYS UNTIL THE ENERGY IS ALL GONE.

HOW LONG DOES IT TAKE FOR A RADIOACTIVE METAL TO LOSE ALL ITS ENERGY? THE ANSWER DIFFERS FOR EACH METAL. SOME METALS LOSE ENERGY QUICKLY—IN ONLY A FEW MINUTES, HOURS, OR DAYS. OTHER METALS, LIKE RADIUM, CAN TAKE A VERY LONG TIME TO LOSE THEIR ENERGY. SCIENTISTS USE THE TERM "HALF-LIFE" TO DESCRIBE HOW LONG IT TAKES FOR AN

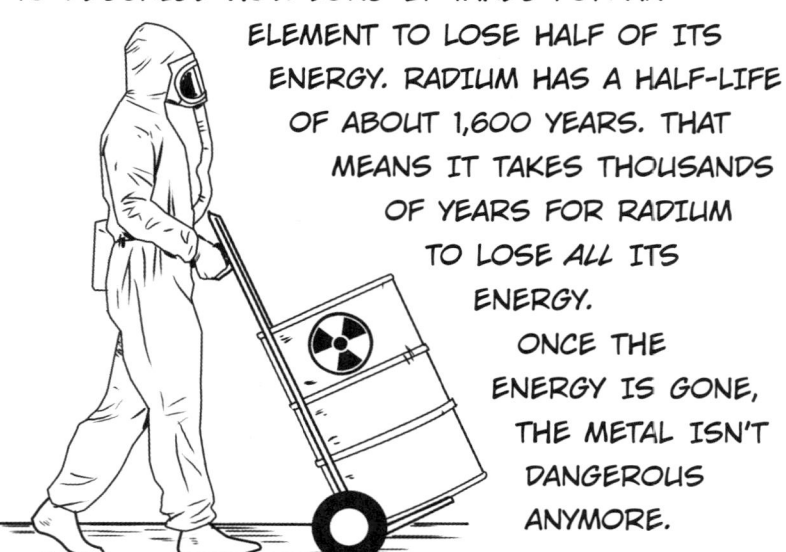

ELEMENT TO LOSE HALF OF ITS ENERGY. RADIUM HAS A HALF-LIFE OF ABOUT 1,600 YEARS. THAT MEANS IT TAKES THOUSANDS OF YEARS FOR RADIUM TO LOSE ALL ITS ENERGY.

ONCE THE ENERGY IS GONE, THE METAL ISN'T DANGEROUS ANYMORE.

She had to hurry! Now that the world knew about polonium, other scientists might want to study it. Even Becquerel was interested in Marie's work. In those days, just like today, scientists tried to help one another, but they also competed with one another to be the first with new ideas.

Becquerel was both a friend and a competitor. He helped Marie get some money for her experiments, but instead of telling Marie about the money, he told Pierre! He treated her like she wasn't as important as Pierre because she was a woman. Becquerel also took ideas from Marie's work and tried to do similar experiments himself.

Pierre was totally the opposite. He didn't like to compete. He simply loved science for its own sake. Marie was the ambitious one. She wanted credit for her discovery. She was determined to be first to prove that her new metal existed.

Marie got to work. She tried to separate the polonium from the pitchblende—but she failed.

The amounts of polonium in the pitchblende were too tiny.

While she was trying, though, she stumbled onto something else. Something even better! The pitchblende contained another mysterious metal that was giving off rays. This one was even more radioactive than polonium. What was it?

Marie did a series of tests to find out. After several experiments, she realized she had found another new element! She and Pierre named this new metal radium. Radium was so powerful that even the tiniest amount was a million times more radioactive than uranium.

It was an amazing year for Marie and Pierre. By December 1898, she had discovered two new chemical elements that the world hadn't known about! Other scientists were beginning to notice her work.

However, some scientists still wanted more proof. They weren't sure she was right. They wanted to see the radium, and touch it.

Was it even possible to separate the radium from the pitchblende?

Marie was determined to try.

Chapter 6
It Glows!

Now that Marie was a little bit famous, she hoped the scientific world would show her some respect. She and Pierre asked the Sorbonne for a bigger, better laboratory. They wanted a clean space with new equipment so she could continue her work.

The Sorbonne refused.

Instead, they said she could take over a huge, dirty, leaky, old building near the college. The building had been used by medical students to cut up dead bodies for experiments!

There was no heat in her lab. In the winter, the place was horribly cold. Marie and Pierre had to huddle around a small stove to keep warm, sipping cups of tea.

Some days Marie forgot to eat, she was so busy
with her work. Some nights, she went home to see
her daughter, but then went back to her lab after
Irene was asleep.

For three long years, Marie sifted through tons
of pitchblende. It was backbreaking work. The
crushed rocks were delivered to the courtyard
outside her lab. She stirred huge amounts of
brown dust in a giant pot with other chemicals.
She had to boil the mixture, then wash it to
separate out the metals. It took fifty tons of water
to wash one ton of crushed rocks! All together,
Marie used eight tons of pitchblende and four
hundred tons of water before she was done!

Little by little, Marie was succeeding. She

was getting tiny amounts of radium out of the pitchblende. At first it wasn't pure radium. It was just something called radium salts, but she kept working, trying to get a purer form of the metal.

The radium salts gave off a lovely glow each night in the dark lab. Marie and Pierre brought a glass jar of it home to keep beside their bed. They liked to watch it glow in the dark.

Marie didn't know it at the time, but handling

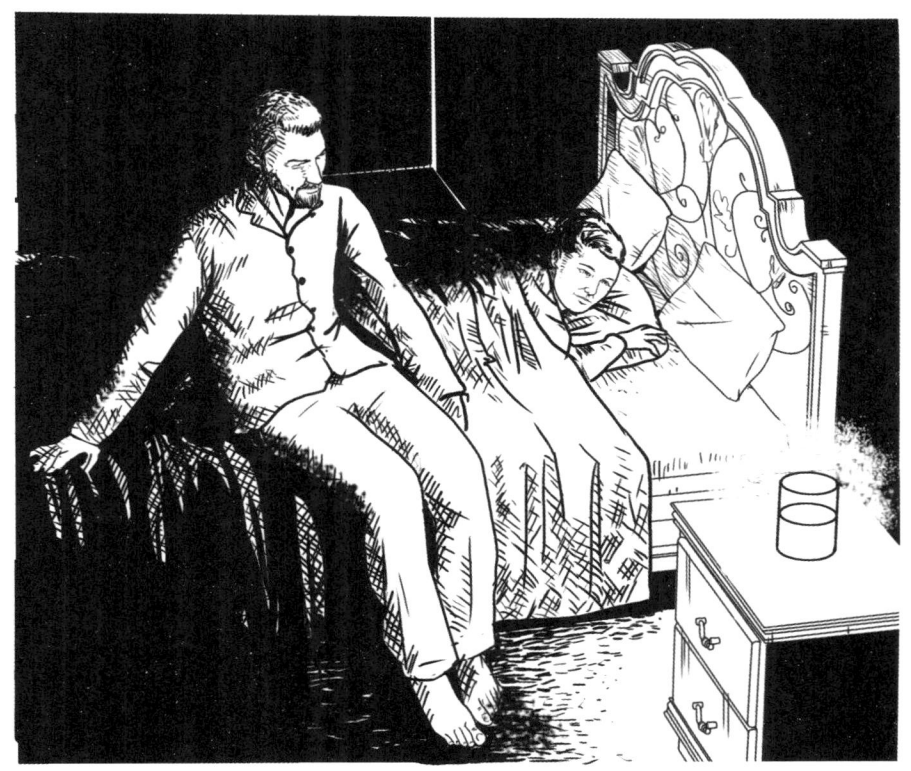

radium wasn't a good idea. The rays it gave off were dangerous. Touching it damaged her skin, although slowly. Henri Becquerel had carried a glass tube of radium salts around in his jacket. A few weeks later, his skin was burned in the spot where the radium had been. Pierre found the same thing happened to him. Being around radium damaged the insides of their bodies, too. It was making them sick.

Still, Marie kept working and writing research reports about her discoveries. Sometimes she and Pierre wrote them together. Marie and Pierre were still not fully respected. Often, Becquerel was given more attention and respect. It must have been hard to work side by side with Becquerel, especially when Pierre thought that Becquerel was secretly trying to keep him out of the Academy of Sciences.

Finally in July 1902, after nearly four years, Marie had a few grains of pure radium! It was enough to prove it really existed. Other scientists tested the metal and agreed she was right.

Marie wrote another long research paper about her discovery. With this report, she could now get her PhD from the Sorbonne. Marie had never cared about clothes, but she bought a new dress for the occasion. In June 1903, she had a celebration dinner. Besides Pierre, several friends and famous scientists joined her, including Gabriel Lippmann. They were all so proud of her.

SPECTROSCOPES: HOW NEW METALS ARE IDENTIFIED

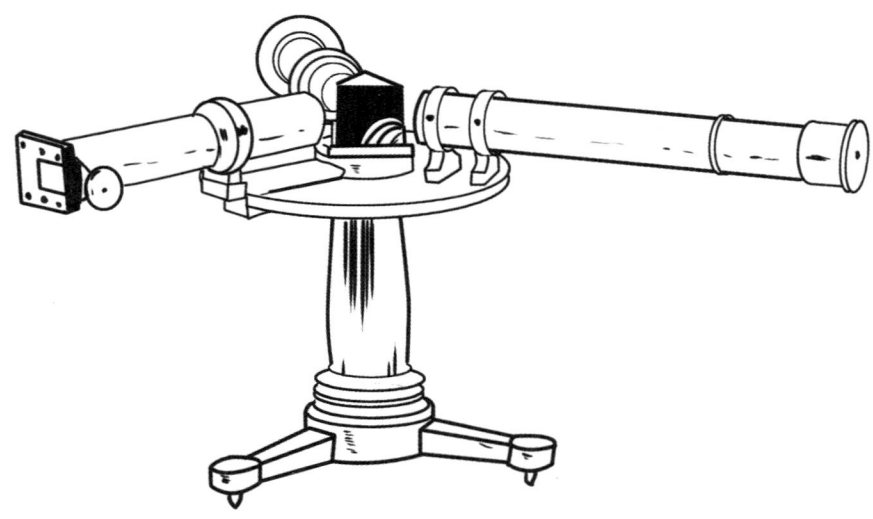

EVERY PURE CHEMICAL ELEMENT IS UNIQUE. THIS IS TRUE FOR METALS, TOO, BECAUSE METALS ARE CHEMICAL ELEMENTS.

TO IDENTIFY A CHEMICAL, SCIENTISTS HEAT IT UP ENOUGH TO MAKE IT GLOW. THEN THEY LOOK AT THE GLOWING LIGHT WITH A TOOL CALLED A SPECTROSCOPE. A SPECTROSCOPE CAN SEE A RAINBOW PATTERN OF COLORS COMING FROM THE GLOWING LIGHT. THE RAINBOW PATTERN OF LIGHT IS CALLED A SPECTRUM.

THE GLOW FROM EVERY ELEMENT CREATES ITS OWN UNIQUE PATTERN OR SPECTRUM—SORT OF LIKE A FINGERPRINT. IF SCIENTISTS SEE A PATTERN THEY'VE NEVER SEEN BEFORE, THEY KNOW IT'S A BRAND-NEW ELEMENT!

WHEN MARIE CURIE DISCOVERED RADIUM, SHE KNEW THE METAL EXISTED, EVEN THOUGH SHE COULDN'T SEE IT! THE ONLY WAY TO *PROVE* IT EXISTED WAS TO PUT THE RADIUM UNDER A SPECTROSCOPE. IT TOOK MARIE MORE THAN THREE YEARS TO GET ENOUGH RADIUM FOR THE TEST.

Now Marie and Pierre hoped that they would both be able to get good jobs with a decent laboratory. That's all they wanted: a clean, quiet place to work. But they were about to receive something even more exciting. They were about to win the Nobel Prize!

Chapter 7
Fame and Fortune

The Nobel Prize is the highest honor a scientist can receive today. However, when Marie and Pierre received the letter saying they had won, it didn't give them very many details. It didn't say the king of Sweden would be there to hand out the award, and it didn't tell them that they would be getting a huge amount of money—worth more than half a million dollars today!

So Pierre did something shocking. He wrote back to the Nobel Prize committee and said they couldn't come! He thanked them for the prize and explained that Marie was sick. The trip was too long, he said. They couldn't possibly take the time to travel to Sweden. They were too busy teaching their classes.

Pierre and Marie probably didn't realize they were being rude. They also didn't know what a big deal the Nobel Prize was. The prize had only been around for three years.

The Curies were supposed to share the Nobel Prize with one other scientist, Henri Becquerel. Becquerel went to Sweden and accepted the award instead. When he gave his speech, he made it sound like he had done all the work. He hardly mentioned Marie and Pierre at all.

Still, the Curies became famous overnight.
All the newspapers wrote about them. People
were fascinated by Marie—a woman scientist!
Newspaper reporters came to her house day after
day. When Marie wasn't home, the reporters
talked to her daughter, Irene. They even wrote
stories about the cat!

The newspapers called Marie "Madame Curie." *Madame* is the French word for "Mrs." In a way, they were saying that Marie was only Pierre Curie's wife—not famous on her own. Marie was known as Madame Curie for the rest of her life.

Pierre hated the publicity. He hated anything that kept him from his work. For weeks, Marie and Pierre tried to avoid the reporters. When asked questions, they answered with just single words. "Yes." "No."

One good thing came out of their fame. Now the Sorbonne was willing to give Pierre a job as a professor. Also, after all their years of begging, he and Marie were finally given a better lab.

Meanwhile, the whole world was falling in love with radium. Why? Because it glowed in the dark! The glow seemed like a magic potion to many. People imagined it would cure illnesses—and they were partly right. Radium could help treat cancer, but the opposite was also true. Radium was making people sick, including Marie and Pierre.

Rich people foolishly drank radium water every day until their jawbones broke into pieces! Actors and dancers put radium on their costumes so they would glow in the dark.

Radium was painted on watches and clocks so the hands would glow. One makeup company even put radium in their lipstick! All these radium products were hurting people.

Radium hurt Marie and Pierre most of all because they handled it for so many years. Pierre's hands were so damaged that he couldn't even dress himself. His bones ached. Pain made it hard for him to walk.

Marie was often weak, too. But by 1904, she was healthy enough to have another baby! On December 6, a baby girl was born. They named her Eve.

For several months after winning the Nobel Prize, Marie and Pierre enjoyed life. They took vacations to the seashore. They bought some new clothes with their prize money, and ate a few fancy dinners out. Big chunks of the money were sent to Marie's family in Poland. Life seemed good.

Then one day in April 1906, something terrible happened—something that turned Marie's life upside down forever.

Chapter 8
Misery

It was rainy, gray, and damp all over Paris on April 19, 1906. Pierre had gone out to a science meeting that morning. He was in a wonderful mood. His friends said he was happier and talked more than ever before.

After the meeting, Pierre went back out into the rain. There were horses, carriages, cars, people, and trams everywhere. As Pierre began to cross a big, busy street, a huge horse-drawn wagon hit

him. Pierre tried to grab on to the horse, to steady himself, but he was weak. He fell. The wagon driver couldn't stop the heavy cart. The wheel ran over Pierre and crushed his skull.

A few hours later, Marie heard the terrible news that her husband was dead. It struck her as hard as the wagon that killed Pierre. Marie felt as if there was no reason to be happy ever again. She became silent. She wouldn't eat and barely got out of bed. It seemed to her as if her life was over.

For many months, Marie was miserable and alone. She later wrote that her children, Irene and Eve, were her only reasons to go on living.

After a while, the Sorbonne invited Marie to take over Pierre's teaching job. Marie agreed, but it was a bittersweet triumph. While Pierre was alive, they would not let her be a professor! No woman

had ever taught at the Sorbonne. Now that Pierre was dead, she was welcome to take his place.

On the November day in 1906 when Marie arrived to teach her first class, hundreds of people lined the streets. Reporters and photographers came. The crowds waited to hear what the famous Madame Curie would say. Would she mention

Pierre? Would she talk about how much he meant to the world of science? No. Marie simply began the science lesson where Pierre had left off. Even so, people in the audience cried. They all sensed how Marie felt, and how hard it was for her to go on without him.

For the next few years, Marie was sad. Still, she continued her work and moved her children to a house in the country, not far from Paris. Marie wanted Irene and Eve to be able to swim and play outside. She also wanted them to learn. Irene was especially smart and, like Marie, loved math and science. Eve was good at music.

Marie arranged with her friends to teach a small group of their children at home. It was something like the Flying University! All the adults took turns teaching classes in one another's houses.

Marie's friends were all scientists. They all spent time together, having dinner and teaching the children. They went on vacation to the beach together. They were very close.

One day, her friends noticed a change in Marie. Suddenly, she seemed happier! She was wearing a pretty dress with a flower, instead of the black dresses she had been wearing to mourn Pierre.

Pretty soon, her friends figured out why Marie was happy. She had fallen in love! The only problem was that the man she loved—Paul Langevin—was already married.

Paul was part of Marie and Pierre's circle of friends. He had been Pierre's student. He was a brilliant scientist and a good friend. Paul was unhappily married. Sometimes his wife was violent. Paul wished he hadn't married her.

PAUL LANGEVIN

Marie probably never wanted to fall in love with a married man. But she followed her heart and spent time with him anyway. It was the first happiness she had felt in years.

Paul wrote love letters to Marie, and she wrote

back to him. One day, Paul's wife, Jeanne, found the letters. She was furious. She threatened to kill Marie! She even followed Marie in the street!

Marie tried to convince Paul to leave his wife and get a divorce. Paul had four children with Jeanne. He didn't want to break up his family. Finally, he promised his wife that he wouldn't see Marie again—except as a friend.

That year, Marie was on the verge of making history—again. She was nominated to become the first woman member of the French Academy of Sciences. Was France ready to treat women equally? There were strong feelings on both sides. Many newspapers wrote angry articles about it. They thought women should not be allowed into this private group of male scientists. Even though Marie was already one of the most famous scientists in the world, they thought she should be kept out.

FRENCH ACADEMY OF SCIENCES

When it came time to vote, Marie was not even allowed inside the Academy's building to see what happened!

The vote was held at exactly four o'clock on January 24, 1911. Marie was not elected. Her friends were angry about it, but Marie acted like she didn't care. She was not the kind of person to make a fuss about anything.

Besides, Marie still had her work, and she was still in love with Paul.

In November 1911, Marie went to a very

important science meeting in Brussels, Belgium.
All the most famous scientists from Europe were
there, including Albert Einstein. Paul Langevin
went, too.

When Paul's wife found out he and Marie
were in Brussels together, she was furious.
She suspected that Paul and Marie were still
in love. She sent Marie's love letters to the

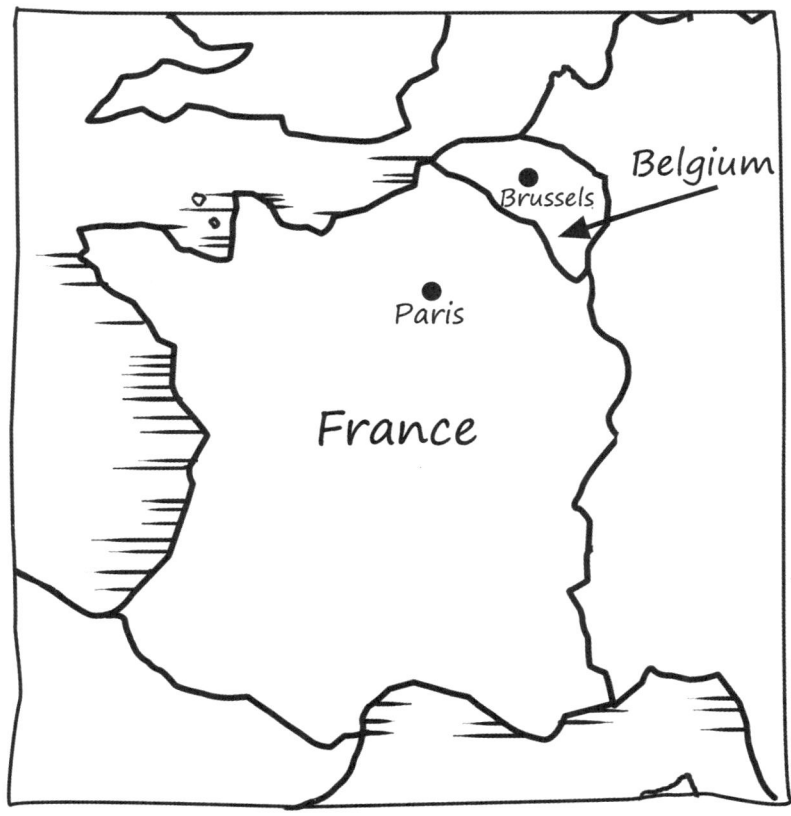

Paris newspapers! A terrible scandal broke out. There were stories about Marie and Paul in the newspaper every day. Many French people thought Marie was to blame.

Marie was angry and horrified. She didn't want her daughters to suffer from the bad publicity. She didn't want it to ruin her career, either.

It was an especially bad time for this kind of trouble. That same week, Marie had just gotten a letter from the Nobel Prize committee. They were giving her *another* Nobel Prize! This time, she alone would be the winner. It was an amazing honor. Only three other people have ever won the Nobel Prize *twice*!

Marie was afraid that the newspaper stories would somehow spoil the Nobel Prize. She was right.

A few weeks later, the Nobel Prize committee sent her a second letter. After all the newspaper stories, they wanted Marie to refuse the prize!

They asked her not to come to Stockholm.

Marie was not going to miss out on this chance to make history. She told the committee that her private life was private. She was coming to Stockholm and accepting the prize. Marie believed they were giving her the Nobel Prize for science—nothing else. Nothing else should matter.

In December 1911, Marie sat in a room with the king of Sweden. The king gave her the

solid gold medal. Marie held her head high and made a speech. A fancy banquet was served with artichokes, fish, chicken, and wine. Her daughter Irene and her sister Bronia were there to share her joy.

It was a thrilling experience for them all, and fourteen-year-old Irene would remember it all her life. It wouldn't be the last time Irene would make that special trip to Stockholm.

Chapter 9
A Family of Scientists

Winning her second Nobel Prize must have been wonderful for Marie, but the terrible scandal with Paul Langevin had taken a toll on her. She was worn out in every way—sick, sad, and depressed. The radium poisoning was probably still making her weak. She had other illnesses, too.

For the next few years, Marie went into hiding. Her love affair with Paul was over, but the world wouldn't forgive her for it. People threw stones at her windows. The newspapers kept writing stories about her.

Marie couldn't bear all the bad things people were saying. She traveled from place to place, leaving her children behind with a governess. Marie used fake names wherever she went. She

didn't want people to know who she was. If someone recognized her and asked, "Are you Madame Curie?" she would lie and say no.

Finally, after a long rest in England with a good friend, Marie felt better. She went back to Paris and back to work.

As time passed, people forgot about the scandal. Once again, she was able to just be herself and do her work. Irene was growing up, too. She and Marie were becoming partners. They talked about science together, just like Marie and Pierre had.

In 1914, a whole building was built for Marie's research. At first it was called the Radium Institute, but later it was renamed the Curie Institute. Marie hoped that she and Irene would work there together there very soon.

Before the lab opened, World War I broke out. The Germans invaded France. Marie wanted to help. She decided her first job was to take all the radium in France and hide it! She didn't want the Germans to find it.

Marie put the radium in a heavy suitcase and traveled ten hours by train. She stored the radium in a vault at a college in Bordeaux. Then she returned to Paris, having eaten nothing for a day and a half. When Marie was on a mission, nothing else mattered.

Next, Marie invented a small X-ray machine that could easily be carried to wounded soldiers.

Her machines were called "Little Curies." Marie and seventeen-year-old Irene drove the machines to hospitals near the battlefields.

WORLD WAR I

THE FIRST WORLD WAR BEGAN IN 1914. IT STARTED WHEN AUSTRIA-HUNGARY FIRED THE FIRST SHOTS. PRETTY SOON, MANY COUNTRIES IN EUROPE WERE FIGHTING ONE ANOTHER. FRANCE, ENGLAND, AND RUSSIA WERE ALL ON THE SAME SIDE. THEY FOUGHT AGAINST GERMANY AND AUSTRIA-HUNGARY. THE GERMANS WERE THE ATTACKERS, MARCHING INTO BELGIUM AND FRANCE TO TAKE OVER.

IN 1917, THE UNITED STATES JOINED THE WAR TO HELP SAVE ENGLAND AND FRANCE. MORE THAN FOUR MILLION AMERICANS FOUGHT THE GERMANS IN EUROPE. AMERICA, ENGLAND, AND FRANCE WON, DEFEATING GERMANY. THE WAR ENDED ON NOVEMBER 11, 1918.

Four years later, after Germany lost the war,
Irene went back to her studies in Paris. Eventually
she graduated and became a scientist, working
alongside Marie.

Then one day, Paul Langevin came back into
their lives in a strange way. Paul told Marie about

a young student of his named Frederic Joliot. Frederic idolized Marie and Pierre Curie. He wanted to work in Marie's lab.

FREDERIC JOLIOT

Marie gave him a job, and soon Frederic fell in love with Irene. At first, Marie didn't trust Frederic. She thought he was just trying to get close to the famous Curie family, but eventually she came to like him. Irene and Frederic Joliot were married on October 9, 1926.

Marie had always suspected that radium could be used to treat cancer, and she was right. She spent the rest of her years working on ways to use radium to help people. At the same time, her daughter and Frederic did their own research. They discovered artificial radioactivity! As Marie grew older and sicker, Irene took over the Radium Institute.

In May 1934, Marie began to feel very weak again. The radium was finally winning out. She was dying. Her daughter Eve took her to the mountains in France, to rest, but it didn't help. Marie died on July 4 at the age of sixty-six.

All of Marie's clothes, books, notebooks, and personal things were too dangerous to touch. They were radioactive! Everything she used in the lab had been affected by the radium. In fact, even after a hundred years, her things were still so radioactive that it wasn't safe to handle them!

When Marie died, she was buried near Pierre in the small French village where he had grown up.

The fame of the great Curie family didn't end there. The very next year, Irene and Frederic Joliot-Curie were given the Nobel Prize for their own discoveries in chemistry.

Irene and Frederic had two children, Helene
and Pierre. They both grew up to be scientists as
well. Amazingly, Helene married Paul Langevin's
grandson, who was also a scientist!

Marie's younger daughter, Eve, wasn't a
scientist. She became a writer instead. She wrote a
book about her mother called *Madame Curie*. Her
book helped make Marie famous in America.

Marie remains the most famous woman in science, even today.

Buildings have been named after her. Two museums are devoted to her life and work. Her picture has been used on money in France and Poland.

In 1995, France decided to dig up Marie's and Pierre's caskets and move them to the Panthéon. The Panthéon is an ancient building in Paris where France's most famous people are

buried. The president of France came for the big ceremony.

At last, it didn't matter that Marie Curie had been a woman. She finally was given the highest possible respect and the honor she had always deserved. Her work had changed the world, and her name would live on forever.

Marie Curie
(1867-1934)

TIMELINE OF
MARIE CURIE'S LIFE

1867 —— Marie Sklodowska is born in Poland

1883 —— Graduates first in her high-school class at age fifteen

1891 —— Arrives in Paris to attend the Sorbonne

1895 —— Marries Pierre Curie

1897 —— Her first daughter, Irene, is born

1898 —— Discovers two new chemical elements

1902 —— Obtains a sample of pure radium

1903 —— Wins the Nobel Prize with Pierre
for their work with radioactivity

1904 —— Pierre begins teaching at the Sorbonne
Her second daughter, Eve, is born

1906 —— Pierre is killed in an accident
Takes over Pierre's teaching job at the Sorbonne

1911 —— Wins her second Nobel Prize

1914 —— Invents an X-ray machine to help wounded soldiers
on the battlefield during World War I

1926 —— Daughter Irene marries Frederic Joliot

1934 —— Dies at the age of sixty-six

TIMELINE OF THE WORLD

The first passenger subway opens in London	1863
President Abraham Lincoln is assassinated	1865
The Suez Canal opens	1869
Alexander Graham Bell invents the telephone	1876
The Brooklyn Bridge opens after over a decade of construction	1883
One of the first silent movies, *The Great Train Robbery*, premieres The Wright brothers fly the first airplane	1903
Henry Ford introduces the Model T	1908
The *Titanic* sinks	1912
World War I begins in Europe The Panama Canal opens Ernest Shackleton journeys to Antarctica	1914
The United States enters World War I	1917
The Treaty of Versailles ends World War I	1919
US stock market crashes, initiating the Great Depression	1929
The Empire State Building is completed	1931
Amelia Earhart becomes the first woman to fly solo across the Atlantic Ocean	1932

BIBLIOGRAPHY

* Cobb, Vicki. **Marie Curie**. New York: DK Publishing, 2008.

Curie, Eve. **Madame Curie: A Biography**. Boston: Da Capo Press, 1937.

Goldsmith, Barbara. **Obsessive Genius: The Inner World of Marie Curie**. New York: Atlas Books, 2005.

Quinn, Susan. **Marie Curie: A Life**. Boston: Da Capo Press, 1995.

* Books for young readers